A CourseGuide for

Church History

Volume One

Everett Ferguson

ZONDERVAN
ACADEMIC

ZONDERVAN ACADEMIC

A CourseGuide for Church History, Volume One: From Christ to the Pre-Reformation

Copyright © 2019 by Zondervan

ISBN 978-0-310-11022-4 (softcover)

Requests for information should be addressed to:
Zondervan, *3900 Sparks Dr. SE, Grand Rapids, Michigan 49546*

Printed in the United States of America

CONTENTS

Introduction

Welcome to *A CourseGuide for Church History, Volume One: From Christ to the Pre-Reformation*. These guides were created for formal and informal students alike who want to engage deeper in biblical, theological, or ministry studies. We hope this guide will provide an opportunity for you to grow not only in your understanding, but also in your faith.

How to Use this Guide

This guide is meant to be used in conjunction with the book *Church History, Volume One* and its corresponding videos, *Church History, Volume One Video Lectures*. After you have read each chapter in the book and watched the accompanying video lesson, the materials in this guide will help you review and assess what you have learned. Application-oriented questions are included as well.

Each CourseGuide has been individually designed to best equip you in your studies, but in general, you can expect the following components. Most CourseGuides begin every chapter with a "You Should Know" section, which highlights key terminology, people, and facts to remember. This section serves as a helpful summary for directing your studies. Reflection questions, typically two to three per chapter, prompt you to summarize key points you've learned. Discussion questions invite you to an even deeper level of engagement. Finally, most chapters will end with a short quiz to test your retention. You can find the answer key to each quiz at the bottom of the page following it.

For Further Study

CourseGuides accompany books and videos from some of the world's top biblical and theological scholars. They may be used independently, or in small groups or classrooms, offering quality instruction to equip students for academic and ministry pursuits. If you would like to engage in further study with Zondervan's CourseGuides, the full lineup may be viewed online. After completing your studies with *A CourseGuide for Church History, Volume One: From Christ to the Pre-Reformation*, we recommend moving on to *A CourseGuide for Church History, Volume Two: From Pre-Reformation to the Present Day*, *A Course-Guide for Historical Theology*, and *A CourseGuide for Systematic Theology*.

CHAPTER 1

The Setting for the Story's Beginning

You Should Know

- Christianity began in a cultural setting defined by three circles of influence: Roman law and government, Greek culture, and Jewish religion.

- Christian attitudes, practices, and social norms showed the influence of pre-existing cultures, yet were worked out within a distinctively Christian frame of reference.

- Judaism provided the immediate religious context for Christianity.

- Jesus was born under the Roman emperor Augustus.

- During Jesus's ministry in Galilee his principal religious opposition came from the Pharisees.

- The vocabulary, ethical assumptions, thought world, and intellectual options of early Christian theologians were provided by Greek philosophy.

- Roman law is one of Rome's enduring legacies to the Western world.

- During Jesus's ministry in Galilee his principal religious opposition came from the Pharisees over the interpretation of the Law of Moses applied to matters of daily life.

Reflection Questions

1. Describe the basic functions of the Imperial Cult in the Roman Empire.

2. Describe key elements in the impact of Greek philosophy on Christian theology.

3. Describe the chief characteristics of the Jewish background of early Christianity.

Discussion Question

1. Explain how the main circles of influence regarding the political, cultural, and religious context in which Christianity began are crucial to understanding the setting for the Christian story's beginning, particularly how they work together.

Quiz

1. (T/F) For early disciples, Latin language and culture were more significant than Greek.

2. (T/F) The Jewish Scriptures were the Bible of the early church.

3. (T/F) The organization of the Roman Empire provided a pattern for the development of the church's hierarchy.

4. (T/F) All of Jesus's first disciples were Jewish.

5. (T/F) Jesus was born in Jerusalem but crucified in Rome.

6. (T/F) The Jewish world in which Jesus was born had not been influenced by Hellenistic culture.

7. (T/F) Christians continued to observe the funerary customs of pre-Christian culture.

8. Which of these items of early Christian belief originally took their meaning from Jewish hopes?

   a) Jesus as the Messiah
   b) A new age of forgiveness of sins
   c) The gift of the Holy Spirit
   d) All of the above

9. During the era of Christianity's beginnings, the social lives of most people were guided by:

    a) The great philosophical systems of Plato and Aristotle
    b) A combination of Roman legal and Greek societal norms
    c) Jewish wisdom literature and the Law of Moses
    d) Astrological practices

10. Which of the following does NOT apply to the Imperial Cult?

    a) It was commonly practiced in Hellenistic Jewish contexts
    b) It helped ensure political unity and loyalty in the empire
    c) It gave divine honor to the emperor and his family
    d) It was often allied with local civic cults

CHAPTER 2

Jesus and the Beginnings of the Church

You Should Know

- Christianity developed within the community of Jesus's earliest disciples on the basis of core Jewish beliefs, as interpreted and exemplified according to Jesus's teaching, ministry, crucifixion, and resurrection.

- The most significant controversy in the very early Christian church concerned the terms by which Gentiles would be accepted into the community.

- With the church's expansion from Jerusalem, traditions about the work of particular apostles became associated with specific locales by the end of the first century, most notably: James in Jerusalem; Peter and Paul in Rome; John in Ephesus; and Thomas in Syria.

- Early Christianity was not uniform, yet a common faith in Jesus and a common core of apostolic traditions helped shape a specifically Christian set of doctrinal commitments, worship practices, and ethical expectations.

- Strong early traditions report that John and Mary came to live in Ephesus.

- James, the brother of Jesus, became a prominent leader of the church in Jerusalem.

- According to strong tradition, Nero was emperor when Paul was beheaded.

- Entrance into the first-century Christian community required faith in Jesus as Lord and Savior and baptism (in his name).

Reflection Questions

1. Compare and contrast first-century Jewish beliefs and practices with those of the early church.

2. Explain the arguments in support of the traditional associations of Peter and Paul with the church at Rome.

3. Discuss the role and impact of Jesus's apostles on the formation of the church in different places.

Discussion Question

1. Describe the diversity of first-century Christianity, along with the core aspects of early Christian beliefs and practices that were uniting factors.

Quiz

1. (T/F) Roman crucifixion was normally reserved for people who were judged to be religious subversives.

2. (T/F) In the areas of religious practice and ethics, the early church broke radically with traditional Jewish institutions.

3. (T/F) The historical evidence that Peter was martyred in Rome is strong.

4. (T/F) Affirmations of Jesus's atoning death and his resurrection were the two pillars of early Christian faith.

5. (T/F) The lack of uniformity in early Christianity is marked by the stark differences in core beliefs and widely divergent moral and worship practices from place to place.

6. (T/F) At the end of the first century, the church in Ephesus appears to have been larger and more influential than the churches in Rome or Jerusalem.

7. Which apostle is often called the "second founder" of Christianity?

    a) Peter
    b) James
    c) John
    d) Paul

8. What function did the "trophies of the apostles" serve?

    a) They identified a person as a true and authoritative apostle
    b) They marked the sites of the martyrdoms of Peter and Paul in Rome
    c) They have helped confirm the association of the apostle Thomas with Syria
    d) They described the eternal rewards awaiting Christians who were martyred

9. Which of the following was NOT a uniting factor in early Christianity?

    a) Interpreting Scripture in light of new revelation in Jesus the Messiah
    b) Rejection of large portions of the Hebrew Scriptures
    c) Sunday assemblies
    d) The Lord's Supper

10. What was the most significant controversy in the very early church?

    a) The terms of acceptance of Gentiles into the Christian community
    b) The question of apostolic authority and the canon of scripture
    c) The question of Jesus's divinity
    d) Defining correct worship practices and moral principles

CHAPTER 3

The Subapostolic Age

You Should Know

- "Jewish Christianity" became less prominent during the subapostolic era due to mutual rejection of each other by many Gentile and Jewish believers, though distinctive strands of Jewish Christianity persisted briefly in such groups as the Ebionites, Nazoreans, and Elkesaites.

- The so-called "Apostolic Fathers" consist of a loose corpus of texts in different genres composed in the subapostolic era, addressing various issues of identity, moral practice, and church life.

- Apocryphal literature and other forms of early Christian literature attest to the range of popular piety and doctrinal convictions of early Christian communities.

- Debate exists as to whether the subapostolic literatures are best understood as testifying to the decay in the vitality of apostolic faith or simply as distinct adaptations to changing circumstance.

- Jewish Christianity: sometimes used broadly to cover all characteristically Jewish influences on Christianity and sometimes used to refer to Christianity among ethnic Jews; narrowed further in the church fathers to refer to those Jewish Christians regarded by the Gentile church as heretical because of their adherence to distinctively Jewish religious observances

- Ebionites: group of Jewish Christians most commented on by Gentile Christian writers, and treated by them as heretical

- Apocrypha: additional Christian writings beyond the New Testament in the second century, and remains an important source for assessing the variety of expressions of popular piety in the early church

• *Didache*: a manual of church life

Reflection Questions

1. Describe some examples of early Christian apocryphal literature, discussing their apparent purposes and functions in early communities of faith.

2. Compare and contrast the basic qualities of the surviving second- and third-generation Christian literature with the literature of the New Testament.

3. Discuss the use and significance of the subapostolic literature for understanding the development of Christianity after the apostolic era.

Discussion Question

1. Choose either: *Didache*, *Epistle of Barnabas*, *1 Clement*, or the *Letters* of Ignatius, describing the contents of the selected Apostolic Father, the likely context and circumstances of its origin, and explaining what it says about key developments in early Christianity.

Quiz

1. (T/F) The *Didache* is primarily concerned with the question of how to address sin after baptism.

2. (T/F) By the end of the first century, many synagogues had taken action that effectively removed Christian believers from membership.

3. (T/F) Polycarp wrote a series of letters on his way from Antioch to face trial in Rome.

4. (T/F) Peter, Paul, and James, the brother of Jesus were all killed within five years of each other.

5. (T/F) Some of the Apostolic Fathers overlap in time with the later New Testament writings.

6. (T/F) *Gospel of Thomas* is a passion narrative with docetic leanings.

7. (T/F) Papias expressed a preference for the living voice of oral testimony over what was written in books.

8. Which Apostolic Father consists of *Visions*, *Parables*, and *Commandments*?

   a) *Didache*
   b) *Hermas*
   c) *2 Clement*
   d) Ignatius

9. Which of the following was NOT part of the three-fold congregational ministry Ignatius prescribes as a way to deal with divisiveness?

   a) Presbyters
   b) Bishop
   c) Evangelists
   d) Deacons

10. *1 Clement* illustrates the tendency of the Western church to be concerned with what?

   a) Ascetic piety
   b) Mystical piety and spiritual unity
   c) Rejection of pagan philosophy
   d) Order and practical unity

CHAPTER 4

The Church and the Empire

You Should Know

- Popular opinion responded negatively to Christian aloofness, the strangeness of their beliefs and practices, and Christians' unwillingness to worship pagan gods. Imperial authorities were bothered by the apparent obstinacy of Christian subjects unwilling to show political loyalty by worshipping the emperor and the gods of Rome.

- Roman persecution of the church prior to the mid-3rd century was sporadic and localized, not systematic.

- Christian apologists of the second century responded to both popular and philosophical accusations against Christianity, employing the philosophy and rhetoric of the day in order to rebut accusations and promote Christian belief and practice.

- The *logos* Christology of the second-century apologists supplied Christian intellectuals with a way to address non-Christian concerns about Christian teaching, as well as providing the foundation for later Trinitarian speculation.

- The surviving literature of second-century martyrdom supplied stories and themes that permanently shaped the self-understanding of the Christian church.

- A developing theology of martyrdom was expressed through several characteristic motifs, many of which helped connect the martyr's experience with that of Jesus Christ.

- Christians who were persecuted at Lyons, but not put to death, preferred to call themselves confessors rather than martyrs.

- Tatian wrote the *Oration against the Greeks*, blasting pagan Greek culture for its immorality.

- Justin Martyr composed a dialogue with Trypho, providing important information about the questions at issue between Jews and Christians in the second century.

- In Greek, the term *logos* means both the rational word in the mind and the word on the tongue.

Reflection Questions

1. From the various responses of the second-century Christian apologists, characterize the general response to pagan accusations and suspicions.

2. Compare and contrast the *logos* Christology of the second-century apologists with teachings about Jesus Christ and God's Word in the Bible.

3. In what ways do the apologists mark an important development in the Christian intellectual effort? Illustrate from the surviving evidence.

Discussion Question

1. Describe four of the eight motifs of martyrdom given in the section.

Quiz

1. (T/F) The apologists stressed that Christians are good citizens and pray for the empire.

2. (T/F) Polycarp of Smyrna was eager to present himself for martyrdom.

3. (T/F) Perpetua's father encouraged her to face martyrdom bravely.

4. (T/F) Roman persecution of early Christianity was more a matter of enforcing political allegiance than repressing a novel religion.

5. (T/F) Early Christians were accused of cannibalism.

6. (T/F) The emperor Nero instigated the first systematic, empire-wide persecution of Christians.

7. Which of the following was NOT a major motif of early Christian martyrdom theology?

   a) Purification by fire
   b) Baptism
   c) Eucharist
   d) Athletes and heroes

8. Under which of the following emperors did Christians suffer a great deal, due to a series of disasters and misfortunes throughout the Roman world?

   a) Marcus Aurelius
   b) Domitian
   c) Nero
   d) Trajan

9. Which early Christian affirmation about the *logos* was NOT to be found in either the Jewish or Greek backgrounds to the concept?

   a) The *logos* is in the mind of God
   b) The *logos* is immanent in the world
   c) The *logos* is the spoken word of God
   d) The *logos* became incarnate in a specific historical person

10. Which of the following composed an extended intellectual attack on Christianity that received major treatment by Origen?

   a) Lucian of Samosata
   b) Celsus
   c) Marcus Aurelius
   d) Pliny the Younger

ANSWER KEY

1. T, 2. F, 3. F, 4. T, 5. T, 6. F, 7. A, 8. A, 9. D, 10. B

CHAPTER 5

Heresies and Schisms in the Second Century

You Should Know

- Early Christianity was characterized by a certain variety in belief and practice.

- A strategic and gifted administrator, Marcion led an effective movement that rejected Christianity's Jewish roots, distinguished the creator god from the redeemer god, emphasized asceticism, and advocated an authoritative canon of Scripture based mainly on portions of Paul's writings.

- In the second century, Gnostic movements developed systems of belief that interacted and competed with catholic Christianity, combining Jewish, Christian, and pagan beliefs.

- In an attempt to achieve a philosophical-religious solution to the problem of evil, Gnostic groups taught complex cosmologies that tended to involve extreme dualism, a strong rejection of matter as evil, and redeemer myths.

- In rejecting Gnosticism, "orthodox" Christianity affirmed the oneness of God, the essential goodness of creation, the full incarnation of Jesus Christ, and bodily resurrection.

- Largely in response to perceived worldliness and formalization of the church, Montanism arose as an exuberant movement stressing prophecy, rigorous ethics, and eschatological enthusiasm.

- Encratism describes a tendency in some Christian circles towards extreme asceticism.

- The appeal to existing standards of belief and practice suggests that "orthodoxy" in some sense existed prior to Christian "heresy."

- The Greek term *gnosis* means knowledge.

- Montanism: another name for the New Prophecy or the Phrygian Heresy

Reflection Questions

1. Compare and contrast Marcion and Valentinus, in terms of their contexts, beliefs, and impact.

2. Identify two influential Gnostic teachers, explaining circumstances of their contexts and the particulars of their beliefs.

3. In what ways were Gnostic beliefs suited to the culture of the second and third centuries?

Discussion Question

1. On what basis might one argue that orthodoxy preceded heresy? Explain.

Quiz

1. (T/F) In response to Gnostic devaluation of matter, orthodox Christianity stressed the full incarnation of Jesus Christ.

2. (T/F) Encratites were accused of becoming drunk on the wine of the Eucharist.

3. (T/F) The teacher Marcion was a wealthy ship-builder.

4. (T/F) Valentinus and his followers were gifted biblical exegetes.

5. (T/F) The oldest known fixed collection (i.e. canon) of New Testament books was defined by Marcion.

CHAPTER 6

The Defense against Rival Interpretations

You Should Know

- Partly in response to internal and external pressures, the early church developed a three-fold defense of what is apostolic: the episcopate, the rule of faith and creed, and the canon.

- The monepiscopacy grew out of practical leadership concerns and came to be associated with the idea of apostolic succession.

- The rule of faith and the creed were received as summaries of the apostolic teaching, for instruction and liturgical use.

- The Apostles' Creed grew out of an earlier formula of baptismal confession used in Rome, attesting to an early practice of regularly reciting in worship a concise statement outlining key tenets of orthodox Christian belief.

- The formation and recognition of the New Testament canon underwent four stages: Scripture principle, canonical principle, closed canon, and recognition of the closed canon; several criteria of canonicity functioned in an interrelated way.

The church did not create the canon but recognized it, putting itself under the authority of Scripture.

he bishop Ignatius is the earliest attestation to a single bishop at e head of the presbytery.

esippus drew up the lists of bishops in different cities that aeus used in his discussion of apostolic succession.

- Second-century Christian three-fold biblical witness: the prophets, the Lord, and the apostles

- The Rule of Faith: the flexible early summary of the apostolic teaching

Reflection Questions

1. Describe and explain the development of the monepiscopacy.

2. Explain the early Christian need to identify and define "apostolicity," illustrating from the developments of episcopacy, creed, and canon.

3. Discuss the differences between the rule of faith and the creed, explaining their respective functions in the early church.

Discussion Question

1. Describe each of the four stages in the development of the canon. Either defend or argue against the claim that the church did not create the canon but recognized it.

Quiz

1. (T/F) The most important criterion for recognizing the canonicity of a book was its inspiration.

2. (T/F) In addition to being in the proper apostolic succession, bishops were expected to manifest sound doctrine and a holy life in order to be respected as authoritative.

3. (T/F) The Apostles' Creed came to be used universally throughout the western and eastern branches of the church.

4. (T/F) Some of the terminology in the Apostles' Creed reflects points at issue in the conflict with heretics.

5. (T/F) The idea of a Christian canon was established before the third century.

6. (T/F) The *Muratorian Fragment* included *Apocalypse of Peter* in its canon.

7. Which criterion for canonicity involves a book's applicability to the whole church?

    a) Widespread reading in worship
    b) Right doctrine
    c) Apostolicity
    d) Catholicity

8. Which of the following books was disputed by many into the fourth century, as reported by Eusebius?

    a) Gospel of Matthew
    b) Jude
    c) 2 Corinthians
    d) Gospel of Peter

9. What statement best describes the early church's relationship to the canon?

    a) The church placed itself under the authority of the canon
    b) The organized church determined the shape and content of the canon
    c) The church formulated the canon in reaction to heretical books and "false canons"
    d) The church relied more on the rule of faith than on the canon

10. Which of the following composed the first ancient list to correspond exactly to our present list of twenty-seven New Testament books?

    a) Gnostic teachers
    b) Athanasius
    c) Eusebius
    d) Marcion

CHAPTER 7

The Fathers of the Old Catholic Church and Their Problems

You Should Know

- Though diverse and often judged inadequate by later standards, the fathers from the late second and early third centuries sustained the faith and decisively shaped later Christian thought and practice.

- In response to heresy, Irenaeus articulated the premises on which the old catholic church developed.

- Tertullian was the first Latin theologian and had great influence on western Christianity.

- Alexandria was a key Hellenistic Christian center; its teachers Clement and Origen developed the foundations of philosophical Christianity.

- The church struggled to define the nature of the church's holiness, wrestling with problems evident especially in the career of Hippolytus and in conflict regarding the status of the lapsed.

- Debates about liturgical practice (Quartodecimans), church discipline (laxist vs. rigorist), and theology (Monarchianism) animated much theological reflection during the period.

- Due to its leadership, size, location, and role in the controversies of the age, the church at Rome rose in prominence to become the chief church by about the end of the second century.

- In the East, Modalism was commonly known as Sabellianism, after its most important representative.

- *Lapsi*/The Lapsed: Christians who fell away from the church in times of persecution
- *On First Principles*: the church's first systematic theology, composed by Origen

Reflection Questions

1. Describe and explain the development and articulation of views about Christ among the early catholic fathers.

2. Compare and contrast the attitudes and work of Tertullian, on the one hand, with Clement and Origen, on the other.

3. Describe and explain the factors leading to the rise to prominence of the church at Rome.

Discussion Question

1. What was at stake in the dispute between Callistus and Hippolytus? Explain the origin of their conflict and its outcome.

Quiz

1. (T/F) Tertullian wrote in Latin.

2. (T/F) Public confession in church had been abolished by the end of the second century.

3. (T/F) "Recapitulation" in early catholic thought refers to the understanding by which Christians are meant to follow and imitate the actions of Jesus Christ.

4. (T/F) Irenaeus advocated a "double faith" theory.

5. (T/F) Bishop Victor of Rome was unwilling to extend communion to Quartodecimans.

6. (T/F) Dynamic Monarchianism was also known as "Patripassianiam."

7. Who was reputed to have made himself a eunuch for the sake of devotion to Christ?

    a) Irenaeus
    b) Callistus
    c) Tertullian
    d) Origen

8. Who wrote, "What has Athens to do with Jerusalem? What concord is there between the Academy and the church?"

    a) Tertullian
    b) Clement
    c) Hippolytus
    d) Gregory Thaumaturgus

9. Which of the following was considered the "moral" sense of Scripture, according to Origen?

    a) The bodily sense
    b) The pneumatic sense
    c) The anagogical sense
    d) The psychic sense

10. Which of the following held a "laxist" position regarding church discipline?

    a) Novatian
    b) Tertullian
    c) Hippolytus
    d) Callistus

CHAPTER 8

Church Life in the Second and Third Centuries

You Should Know

- After an intensive and often lengthy period of preparation, converts were initiated into Christianity through a highly symbolic baptism ritual.

- Christians were in the habit of meeting on Sundays and other times for worship and instruction; celebrating the Eucharist was central to Sunday gatherings.

- The church was known for advocating high standards of personal morality, including sexual behavior and charity.

- Women were prominent in the story of early Christianity, as celebrated martyrs, in special roles of church service, and defining new social roles through celibacy.

- Christian hope of bodily resurrection supplied a powerful testimony. Christian expectations included chiliastic and non-chiliastic understandings of the end times.

- *Apostolic tradition* required that candidates for baptism receive instruction for a period of three years.

- In approximately the year 200, the church at Rome acquired a cemetery that became the nucleus of the catacomb of Callistus.

- The eschatological view that looked for Christ to rule the earth from Jerusalem for 1,000 years is known as chiliasm.

- In addition to the baptismal Eucharist, persons who were baptized were given milk and honey, symbolizing the food of infants and entrance into the Promised Land.

Reflection Questions

1. Explain the various ways in which baptism was practiced in the first few centuries of the church, illustrating from the early sources.

2. Describe the early Christian practice of the Eucharist and other meals, explaining the fundamental ideas and beliefs that shaped the practices.

3. Evaluate the moral expectations of the early church in light of the common moral expectations of contemporary society. Describe the basic moral habits and expectations of early Christians, taking into account the diversity and development of the first few centuries.

Discussion Question

1. Describe the basic devotional and worship habits of early Christians, taking into account the diversity and development of the first few centuries. Compare and contrast this worship of early Christianity with contemporary Christian worship with which you are most familiar.

Quiz

1. (T/F) Candidates for baptism in the early church removed their clothing in order to be baptized.

2. (T/F) The celebration of the Eucharist was seen to be an argument against heretics who denied the full incarnation of Christ, like Docetists and Gnostics.

3. (T/F) Orthodox eschatology believed in the resurrection of the soul rather than the body.

4. (T/F) Due to the small size and persecuted status of the church,

charity for the poor and the underprivileged was not a strong characteristic of early Christianity.

5. (T/F) Christians in the early church were never allowed to serve in the military.

6. (T/F) By the end of the third century, only the baptized were admitted to the Lord's Supper portion of the service.

7. When did infant baptism become routine?
   a) The first century
   b) The second century
   c) The third and fourth centuries
   d) The fifth and sixth centuries

8. What early Christian document described Christian moral teaching as the "Way of Life?"
   a) *Martyrdom of Polycarp*
   b) *Epistle to Diognetus*
   c) *Didache*
   d) Clement of Alexandria's *Paedagogus*

9. When did it become normal for churches to rent or purchase buildings for their own use?
   a) By the fourth century
   b) By the third century
   c) By the second century
   d) In the first century

10. In what group/s did women engage in public preaching and preside at liturgical functions?
   a) Orthodox churches
   b) Novatianists
   c) Montanists
   d) All of the above

CHAPTER 9

Development of the Church during the Third Century

You Should Know

- After a long history of enduring sporadic persecutions, the mid-third century saw the first systematic persecution of Christianity in the Roman Empire.

- The cult of the martyrs developed in the last half of the third century, strongly impacting corporate and personal spirituality.

- Cyprian of Carthage engaged in a number of disputes regarding church order and discipline, composing treatises and letters that shaped western ecclesiology.

- Christian art and architecture began to flourish from the mid-third century, exhibiting styles and motifs common to the culture yet adapted to biblical stories and Christian purposes (especially funerary).

- Manicheism posed a competitive threat to Christianity from the mid-third century.

- Texts such as *Didascalia Apostolorum* and the work of leaders such as Gregory Thaumaturgus, Methodius, Lactantius, and Dionysius of Alexandria helped shape the church of the last half of the third century.

- The emperor Decius was responsible for launching the first empire-wide persecution on Christianity.

- Important Christian art from the 240s survives in a house converted for use as a church in the city of Dura Europa in Syria.

- Two classes of adherents in the religion of Manicheism: the elect and hearers

- *Didascalia* Apostolorum: the long third-century Syriac text supplying rich information about many facets of church life

Reflection Questions

1. Discuss the circumstances of Christian persecution in the Roman Empire from the late-second through the mid-third century, explaining the effects of persecution on Christian piety (e.g. martyr's cult and Christian art) and church discipline (e.g. the lapsed).

2. Describe the career of Cyprian of Carthage, discussing the major controversies in which he was embroiled and explaining his arguments on aspects of church order and practices of church discipline.

3. What factors do scholars adduce to explain the growth and success of the church in the third century?

Discussion Question

1. Compare and contrast the contributions of Dionysius of Alexandria, Gregory Thaumaturgus, and *Didascalia Apostolorum* to the shape of third-century Christianity.

Quiz

1. (T/F) Though originally acquired as cemeteries, the catacombs proved most useful as hiding places during times of persecution.

2. (T/F) During the persecutions of the third century, some Christians obtained fraudulent certificates to show they had sacrificed to the gods.

3. (T/F) The story of Jonah was the most commonly occurring Old Testament scene in early Christian art.

4. (T/F) Eastern theologians tended to stress the oneness of the God-head.

5. (T/F) By the end of the third century Christians made up a sizable minority of the population of the Roman Empire.

6. (T/F) Christians experienced higher survival rates during the epidemic of the 250s.

7. Which of the following ideas was most difficult for pagans to accept?
   a) Resurrection of the body
   b) High moral standards
   c) Monotheism
   d) All the above were equally difficult for pagans to accept

8. Which author wrote an important treatise called *On the Resurrection*?
   a) Methodius
   b) Gregory Thaumaturgus
   c) Lactantius
   d) Dionysius of Alexandria

9. Cyprian debated with which bishop over the issue of whether to rebaptize former heretics or schismatics?
   a) Novatian of Rome
   b) Dionysius of Alexandria
   c) Stephen of Rome
   d) Dionysius of Rome

10. Which of the following is not a theory advanced to explain the absence of Christian art prior to about 200?
   a) The economic and social circumstances of most Christians
   b) The desire not to attract attention unnecessarily during times of persecution
   c) A continuation of the Jewish aversion to images
   d) All the above are theories advanced to explain its absence

CHAPTER 10

Diocletian and Constantine

On the Threshold of the Fourth Century

You Should Know

- During a period of imperial reform in the late third and early fourth centuries, Christians underwent the most severe and widespread persecution yet.

- Though the person and motives of Constantine the Great are complex and somewhat mysterious, he achieved sole authority in the Roman Empire, ended the persecutions, favored Christianity, and ushered in Christendom.

- The church was largely unprepared for the many challenges accompanying the change in church-state relations.

- The Donatist controversy exemplified the way in which state involvement could affect church affairs, as rigorist and laxist factions faced off in North Africa and experienced the impact of imperial intervention.

- Many bishops met in the first ecumenical council at Nicaea in 325 to debate the theological views of the subordinationist Arius, resulting in the Nicene Creed and signaling new developments in the ways church and state leaders would tackle issues affecting Christianity at large in the Roman Empire.

- The wealthy woman Lucilla was instrumental in causing the schism in Carthage that resulted in the Donatist group.

- The Greek term *homoousios* was put into the creed at Nicaea to stress that the divine Father and the Son share the same substance, against Arius.

- The greatest outward show of Constantine's favoritism towards the church was his extensive program of building/construction.

- In 314, a synod met at Arles to address the Donatist problem.

Reflection Questions

1. Discuss the circumstances of Christian martyrdom in the Roman Empire prior to 313, explaining the Christian response(s) and the effects of persecution on Christian piety, church discipline, etc.

2. Describe and evaluate the impact of Constantine's rise to power on the church and Christianity in the early fourth century.

3. Describe and explain the circumstances surrounding the development of the Donatist controversy.

Discussion Question

1. Describe and explain the circumstances surrounding the Council of Nicaea (325). Explain the major views present at the Council of Nicaea. In what way was Nicaea important for church history?

Quiz

1. (T/F) Constantine took the title of *pontifex maximus*.

2. (T/F) Though the Donatists attracted many followers, they were never the majority in North Africa.

3. (T/F) In the very first measure of the Great Persecution, Galerius and Diocletian took decisive action by requiring all citizens to sacrifice to the gods.

4. (T/F) Under Constantine, Christian bishops were given the privilege of judging civil cases.

5. (T/F) The *Circumcelliones* were armed enforcers of imperial policy, sent to squash the Donatists in North Africa.

6. (T/F) Due to his widespread influence, the bishop of Alexandria was called "pope" in the early fourth century.

7. Which of the following baptized Constantine?

   a) Saint Helena
   b) Hosius of Cordova
   c) Eusebius of Caesarea
   d) Eusebius of Nicomedia

8. Which author and theologian helped construct a political theology in his extensive writings about Constantine?

   a) Majorinus of Carthage
   b) Hosius of Cordova
   c) Eusebius of Caesarea
   d) Eusebius of Nicomedia

9. Rivalry between which two sees helped fuel the Arian controversy?

   a) Rome and Antioch
   b) Antioch and Alexandria
   c) Carthage and Alexandria
   d) Rome and Alexandria

10. Which of the following was an ardent supporter of Arius's teaching?

   a) Alexander of Alexandria
   b) Hosius of Cordova
   c) Eusebius of Caesarea
   d) Eusebius of Nicomedia

CHAPTER 11

The Church in the Fourth Century

Doctrine, Organization, and Literature

You Should Know

- In the period following the Nicene council—and especially after Constantine's death—the Arian controversy continued to create disunity in the fourth-century church, which saw many councils and at least four different major positions on the relation of the Father to the Son.

- Through the work of key figures like Athanasius and the Cappadocian Fathers, and the involvement of sympathetic emperors, Nicene orthodoxy came to be affirmed and generally accepted by the time of the Council of Constantinople (381).

- Throughout the fourth century, church organization became increasingly formal and its clergy more distinct in role and status from laypersons.

- The "great patristic century" (fourth–early fifth centuries) saw the production of great works of lasting influence on the part of several major writers and church leaders—in Greek: Athanasius, Basil of Caesarea, Gregory of Nazianzus, Gregory of Nyssa, and John Chrysostom; in Syriac: Ephraem the Syrian; and in Latin: Ambrose, Rufinus, and Jerome.

- Bishop Ambrose was able to command the penitent submission of the emperor Theodosius I.

- The emperor Theodosius I declared Christianity the faith of the empire in 380.

- A relentless advocate of Nicene orthodoxy, Athanasius was exiled no fewer than five times, depending on the changing political situation.

- Chorepiscopus: a rural bishop supervised by the city bishop

Reflection Questions

1. Compare and contrast four major fourth-century viewpoints on the relationship between the Father and the Son.

2. Analyze the principal phases in the Arian controversy after Nicaea, explaining major themes and identifying major players.

3. Describe the Council of Constantinople, explaining its theological and political background, including the roles played by significant figures.

Discussion Question

1. Select three (3) of the following major patristic figures, comparing their careers, roles, and contributions to Christian thought and practice: Basil of Caesarea, Gregory of Nyssa, John Chrysostom, Ambrose, Rufinus, and Jerome.

Quiz

1. (T/F) The emperor Constantius II tried to revivify paganism in the empire.

2. (T/F) Changes in clerical garments were largely the result of the clergy's failure to keep up with changing fashions in secular life.

3. (T/F) Rufinus's *Life of Antony* was very influential in advertising monastic ideals.

4. (T/F) Jerome knew Hebrew and translated the *Vulgate* from the Hebrew Bible.

5. (T/F) In his preaching, John Chrysostom was quick to accuse corrupt clergy, but would not criticize the royal family.

6. (T/F) The "Nicaeno-Constantinopolitan Creed of 381" is the creed most commonly recited today in churches as the "Nicene Creed."

7. Which of the following parties believed that the Son is unlike the Father?
   a) Homoousians
   b) Homoiousians
   c) Homoeans
   d) Anomoeans

8. Which of the following was NOT a persuasive fourth-century argument for the Nicene Creed?
   a) The number of signatories was 318
   b) The term *homoousios* could be clearly defined and understood
   c) The bishops at the Council of Nicaea were good men
   d) The emperor ratified the creed

9. Which of the following Cappadocians is seen as a great "Christian-izer of Hellenism"?
   a) Basil of Caesarea
   b) Gregory of Nazianzus
   c) John Chrysostom
   d) Gregory of Nyssa

10. Which of the following was also known as the "Harp of the Holy Spirit" for his beautiful theological poetry?
    a) Ephraem the Syrian
    b) Ambrose of Milan
    c) Rufinus
    d) Gregory of Nazianzus

CHAPTER 12

Monasticism, Expansion, Life, and Worship

The Church in the Fourth and Early Fifth Centuries

You Should Know

- Under the influence of key leaders and through a variety of expressions, Christian monasticism shaped Christianity in significant ways.

- The fourth and fifth centuries saw one of the most significant periods in Christian missions, with major expansion occurring in Syria, Persia, Armenia, Georgia, and Ethiopia.

- Although Christianity became the official religion of the Roman Empire in the late fourth century, the Christianization of religious practices, moral behavior, and methods of rule was generally slow and gradual.

- In the aftermath of persecution, the cult of the saints, observing saints' days, the veneration of holy sites, and pilgrimage became major expressions of Christian piety.

- In the fourth century Christian worship became more elaborate and the distinction between laity and clergy more pronounced. In particular, the sacraments of baptism, Eucharist, and chrismation received greater attention and significance.

- Practices of penance, ordination, and the church calendar became more formal and more complex during the fourth and fifth centuries.

- By the fourth century, the three acts that had come to have sacramental significance for the church were baptism, the Eucharist, and chrism.

- In Eastern churches the Eucharist was viewed as an epiphany of the divine, but in the West it was viewed as a sacrifice.

- *Martyria*: shrines commemorating the death places of martyrs

Reflection Questions

1. Compare and contrast different forms of monasticism that became current by the fourth and fifth centuries, describing principal leaders associated with each form.

2. Evaluate the effects on society and the church after Rome made Christianity the official religion of the empire.

3. Describe the growth of Christianity in two of the "national" churches discussed in the section.

Discussion Question

1. Describe the development of the sacraments in the fourth–fifth centuries, focusing on aspects of ritual, rationale, and theology.

Quiz

1. (T/F) Although Christian emperors in the fourth century favored Christians, they did not execute pagans.

2. (T/F) The major fourth-century addition to the Christian calendar was the celebration of Jesus's birth.

3. (T/F) In the fourth and fifth centuries, veneration previously given to martyrs was extended to monks and bishops also.

4. (T/F) Constantine officially entrusted the church with orphan care.

5. (T/F) Syriac Christianity was characterized by its emphasis on schools.

6. (T/F) The practice of burying the dead within churches developed largely because of Christians' habit of venerating saints' relics.

7. Which emperor instituted the strictest measures against Jews?

    a) Theodosius II
    b) Julian
    c) Constantine
    d) Gratian

8. Which monastic expression emphasized community life?

    a) That of the hermit
    b) That of the *laura*
    c) That of the cenobites
    d) That of the anchorites

9. According to Gregory Thaumaturgus, the category of penitents who were associated with the faithful, but did not commune were known as:

    a) Mourners
    b) Kneelers
    c) Bystanders
    d) Restored ones

10. Which of the following was not a significant motif in the literature of early Christian monasticism?

    a) Angelic
    b) Baptismal
    c) Martyr
    d) Priestly

CHAPTER 13

Christological Controversies to Chalcedon (451)

You Should Know

- Each of the four ecumenical councils contributes a distinct piece to the Christian doctrine of the incarnation, functioning to preserve mystery within certain parameters.

- The Antiochene and Alexandrine theological traditions differed in significant ways, producing different interpretations of Nicaea that were difficult to reconcile and triggered widespread Christological controversy.

- The backgrounds and circumstances of the Christological controversies demonstrate the shifts occurring in how major religious conflict would be handled in the late empire. The consequences would include deposition of leaders and condemnation of entire traditions.

- The clash between Nestorius and Cyril in the Council of Ephesus (431), the results of which were played out further in the "Robber Synod" of 449 and the Council of Chalcedon (451), highlighted the terms of debate between the Word-flesh Christology of Antioch and the Word-man Christology of Alexandria.

- Chalcedon established a compromised definition, affirming the two natures (human and divine) in the one person of Jesus Christ.

- Chalcedon and its canons impacted the church's understanding of the role of ecumenical councils, the relationship of monks to the ecclesial hierarchy, and underscored the tensions between Constantinople and Rome as prestigious sees.

- Nestorius's response to the use of the term *Theotokos* helped trigger the controversy in Constantinople that led to the Council of Ephesus (431).

- Gregory of Nazianzus's argument against Apollinarianism was stated well in the aphorism about the incarnation, "What was not assumed was not healed."

- At the Council of Ephesus (431), the contingent from Antioch was delayed, but the presider conducted the council anyway.

Reflection Questions

1. Describe and explain the circumstances surrounding the Council of Chalcedon (451), indicating points of dispute, major players, and theological implications of the issues.

2. Explain the debate between Nestorius and Cyril of Alexandria, highlighting the terms of the debate and discussing the role played by the distinct schools of thought that each represented.

3. Explain the significance of each of the first four ecumenical councils, describing their backgrounds, the theological points at issue, major players, and basic consequences of each.

Discussion Question

1. Choose three (3) of the following on which to briefly compare and contrast their significances for the history of the Christological controversy: Theodore of Mopsuestia, Apollinaris of Laodicea, Eutyches, Cyril of Alexandria, Nestorius, John of Antioch, Theodosius II, Dioscorus, Leo I of Rome, Theodoret of Cyrus.

Quiz

1. (T/F) The Alexandrine tradition gave more attention to the humanity of Jesus Christ.

2. (T/F) Monophysitism was an extreme view that insisted Christ had only one nature.

3. (T/F) The christological controversies signal the decline of the effectiveness of the classical Christian argument from tradition.

4. (T/F) At Chalcedon, the terms *physis* and *natura* were used to talk about the duality of Jesus Christ's being.

5. (T/F) The *Twelve Anathemas* composed by Nestorius explained the Antiochene understanding of Christology and rejected Cyril's views.

6. (T/F) Leo I was in favor of the findings of the "Robber Synod" of 449, and rejected the Chalcedonian Definition of Faith.

7. The Council of Ephesus (431) may be best summed up as affirming what Christian doctrinal understanding?

   a) The oneness of God
   b) The oneness of Christ
   c) The twoness of Christ
   d) The threeness of God

8. Which of the following taught that the divine Logos replaced the human soul or spirit of Jesus?

   a) Apollinaris of Laodicea
   b) Theodore of Mopsuestia
   c) Eutyches
   d) Diodore of Tarsus

9. Who collaborated with John of Antioch after the Council of Ephesus to prepare a compromise formula that allowed for both Antiochene and Alexandrine emphases?

   a) Theodosius II
   b) Leo I

c) Dioscorus

d) Cyril of Alexandria

10. The canons of Chalcedon helped bring what element of the church more firmly under bishops' control?

a) Monks

b) Schools

c) Liturgy

d) Deacons

CHAPTER 14

Augustine, Pelagius, and Semipelagianism

You Should Know

- Augustine of Hippo came to be one of the most influential thinkers in western Christianity, shaped by a variety of life experiences culminating in his dramatic conversion to Christianity.

- Augustine left a voluminous quantity of writings that have become classics in western Christianity, addressing theology, ecclesiology, exegesis, and spirituality.

- In response to Donatism, Augustine formulated influential understandings of the sacraments and the church.

- In response to Pelagianism, Augustine formulated controversial but impactful understandings of divine predestination and election, salvation, and human sexuality.

- Pelagius and Celestius were moralizing reformers whose views on human free will prompted fierce controversy, especially in Rome and North Africa, resulting in their condemnation in multiple councils.

- John Cassian, Vincent of Lerins, and others reacted to Augustine's extreme views on divine election, holding to a position that allows a greater role for human free will in salvation, a view known as "Semipelagianism."

- Augustine wrote the work that became the textbook on the theology of marriage in the Middle Ages.

- Augustine's work *Confessions* not only provides crucial information about his life, but became a religious classic of penetrating spiritual introspection.

- While a professor of rhetoric, the non-Christian Augustine went to hear the city's most famous orator, a bishop named Ambrose.

Reflection Questions

1. Compare and contrast Pelagianism with Augustine's views and with Semipelagianism, indicating major players in the controversy and the fundamental points of contention.

2. Describe Augustine's views on human free will, salvation, and divine election, explaining their development.

3. Explain the development of Augustine's views on ordination, the church, and sacraments in response to Donatism. What were the long-term consequences of his teaching?

Discussion Question

1. Select two (2) of the following works to describe, indicating their authors, the circumstances of their composition, their teachings, and their impact: *Confessions*, *Commonitorium*, *City of God*, *On the Trinity*.

Quiz

1. (T/F) Augustine taught that a sacrament like baptism could be valid, regardless of the administrator's purity or the faithfulness of the church.

2. (T/F) Once Pelagius and Celestius had been condemned, Augustine's views on divine election and human sexuality remained unchallenged for centuries.

3. (T/F) Augustine's views on human free will changed substantially as he engaged different issues troubling the church.

4. (T/F) Augustine used infant baptism as an argument in favor of his views on original sin.

5. (T/F) The Council of Ephesus (431) condemned Pelagius, Celestius, and Julian of Eclanum.

6. (T/F) During the Middle Ages, the two cities in *City of God* were typically understood to be church and state.

7. According to John Cassian's fourfold method of reading the Bible, an interpretation of "Jerusalem" as the Heavenly City would fit which sense?

   a) Allegorical
   b) Tropological
   c) Literal
   d) Anagogical

8. Which of the following is NOT consistent with Augustine's views on salvation, original sin, and human free will?

   a) Because of the fall, humans are not able to do good or even choose good without God's supernatural grace
   b) Original sin is passed on through sexual activity
   c) The stories of the two tax collectors in the Gospels illustrate the possible ways a person may come to salvation
   d) God predestines some people for condemnation

9. After Pelagius and his followers had been banished and excommunicated, who assumed leadership of the Pelagian position?

   a) Augustine of Hippo
   b) Vincent of Lerins
   c) John Cassian
   d) Julian of Eclanum

10. Who constructed the classic statement of the ancient church's doctrine of tradition?

   a) Augustine of Hippo
   b) Vincent of Lerins
   c) John Cassian
   d) Julian of Eclanum

CHAPTER 15

Transitions to the Middle Ages

Germanic Migrations, Doctrinal Developments, and the Papacy

You Should Know

- The church was one of the principal institutions in Western Europe to survive the collapse of the ancient Roman Empire.

- Ulfilas converted many Goths to a Christianity that was largely Arian, and its church exhibited distinctive features of organization, belief, and practice as a result of its Germanic context.

- The movements and conquests of German tribes transformed Western Europe during the fifth and sixth centuries, the most impactful being the Franks under Clovis and the Ostrogoths under Theodoric.

- The Germanic invasions had lasting effects on society and the churches; a number of Christian authors sought to explain the significance of the Germanic conquests in different ways.

- The Augustinian-Pelagian controversy was practically resolved in favor of a "Semiaugustinianism" championed by Caesarius of Arles, a compromise view that would come to dominate the Western medieval theology.

- A combination of circumstances and strong leadership contributed to the elevation of the role of Roman bishop (pope) to a status of primacy among Western bishops.

- The expression *filioque* was added to the creed in 589 at a synod in Toledo.

- The proprietary church *Eigenkirche*: The form of organization in which a church was closely associated with the property and rule of a lay patron is known as that of Ulfilas– the fourth-century missionary to the Goths.

- The synod of Orange approved a "Semiaugustinian" view on salvation and human free will in 529.

Reflection Questions

1. Compare and contrast the relationships that the Franks and Visigoths had with Christianity and the church in the fifth and sixth centuries.

2. Describe and explain the distinctive characteristics of early Germanic Christianity in its beliefs, practices, and church organization.

3. In what ways would Augustine and Pelagius have agreed or disagreed with Caesarius of Arles and the synod of Orange (529) on the matter of human free will and salvation?

Discussion Question

1. How did the bishop of Rome come to be as powerful and significant as it was by the beginning of the sixth century? Discuss the major players and relevant events and circumstances.

Quiz

1. (T/F) The Goths spoke of the Father and Son as being of "one blood."

2. (T/F) Scholars agree that the year 476 marks the beginning of the Middle Ages.

3. (T/F) Leo I may justly be called "the first pope."

4. (T/F) Prosper of Aquitaine was a Semipelagian opponent of Augustinianism.

5. (T/F) Salvian contended that the Germans were morally inferior to the Romans and that God would enable the Romans to regain control of the empire.

6. (T/F) In the early Middle Ages, the church conveyed a sense of "universal authority" that transcended the more limited authority of regional kings.

7. Which of the German tribes came to exercise the most influence in the Western church during the early Middle Ages?

   a) Franks
   b) Ostrogoths
   c) Visigoths
   d) Lombards

8. Which of the following is NOT given as a principal factor producing a new situation for the church?

   a) Constantine
   b) Augustine
   c) Monks and popes
   d) Germanic language

9. Who described the bishop of Rome as the "vicar of Peter"?

   a) Leo I
   b) Damasus
   c) Julius
   d) Innocent I

10. Who devised the *anno domini* system of dating?

   a) Cassiodorus
   b) Isidore of Seville
   c) Dionysius Exiguus
   d) Boethius

Eastern and Western Churches in the Fifth and Sixth Centuries

You Should Know

- After the Councils of Ephesus and Chalcedon, the Eastern church experienced a three-way split between the Church of the East ("Nestorians"), Chalcedonians, and Miaphysites/Henophysites, each with its key leaders and trajectory of later development.

- During the emperor Justinian's reign, the empire experienced its first flourishing of Byzantine culture.

- Justinian sought to achieve unity in the empire, involving himself in the Theopaschite, Origenist, and Three Chapters controversies, without accomplishing lasting theological unity.

- Justinian's Byzantine culture saw marked developments in law, reconquest of territories, architecture, liturgy, art, theology, and popular devotion.

- The monastic legacy of Benedict of Nursia and the "monkish papacy" of Gregory the Great combined to establish structures, practices, and expectations that would characterize ecclesial leadership through the Middle Ages.

- The great liturgies were formalized in the sixth–seventh centuries, with the result that several distinct families were in use in different areas.

- From the time of the barbarian invasions of the fifth century, Eastern and Western expressions of Christianity may be distinguished according to different theological emphases, organization, and engagement with society.

- Zeno promoted the *Henoticon*, an edict of reunion, in an effort to unify Chalcedonians and Henophysites.

- Differences between the Eastern and Western churches may be summed up by saying that the Eastern church did not have a Middle Ages.

- Benedict's Rule: a balanced regimen of a) divine praise, b) spiritual reading, and c) physical work

Reflection Questions

1. Explain the three-way split that occurred in the Christian East after the Councils of Ephesus and Chalcedon, indicating major players and events.

2. Describe the significance of Justinian's reign for the ongoing development of the Christological controversies in the Christian East. What was his legacy and how did Byzantine culture flower under his rule?

3. What are the main differences between Eastern and Western theology, organization, and attitudes regarding church and culture?

Discussion Question

1. Select three (3) of the following figures, comparing and contrasting their contributions to the development of Christianity in the fifth and sixth centuries: Severus of Antioch, Pseudo-Dionysius, Benedict of Nursia, Justinian, Gregory the Great.

Quiz

1. (T/F) The Theopaschite controversy was triggered by the inclusion of a particular phrase in the liturgy.

2. (T/F) Justinian reestablished Roman rule in Italy.

3. (T/F) Gregory supported the idea of purgatory.

4. (T/F) Mariology appeared in the West several centuries in advance of the East.

5. (T/F) The church in Armenia adopted the Henophysite position.

6. (T/F) In the latter years of his reign, Justinian was able to achieve lasting unity between Chalcedonians and Miaphysites.

7. Which of the following texts became a medieval classic, with enormous influence on Western clergy?
   a) *Dialogues*
   b) *Pastoral Rule*
   c) *On Ecclesiastical Hierarchy*
   d) *Communicatio idiomatum*

8. The Fifth Ecumenical Council (553) was primarily concerned with which issue?
   a) The Three Chapters
   b) Evagrian Origenism
   c) Christian theurgy
   d) The Theopaschite controversy

9. Which of the following is NOT one of the factors favoring the creation and use of written liturgies?
   a) Natural tendencies to uniformity in worship language
   b) Unlearned clergy needed guidance
   c) Concern for orthodoxy and fear of heretical doctrines
   d) The precedent and model of written scriptures

10. Who identified three stages in describing God — affirmative, negative, and superlative?
   a) Severus of Antioch
   b) Pseudo-Dionysius
   c) Gregory the Great
   d) Benedict of Nursia

CHAPTER 17

The Eastern Churches from the Seventh to Eleventh Centuries

You Should Know

- The monotheletism promoted by church leaders and emperors as a means by which to accomplish unity was condemned in the Sixth Ecumenical Council, Constantinople III (680–81), defeated by a lasting reticence to revise Chalcedon and by the Christology typified in Maximus the Confessor.

- The rise of Islam and its dramatic spread in the seventh and eighth centuries transformed the shape of the empire, posed significant challenges to the church, and prompted a series of Christian responses.

- The iconoclasm sponsored by military emperors in the eighth and ninth centuries was refuted in the Seventh Ecumenical Council, Nicaea II (787), defeated by popular piety and by the incarnational theology typified in John of Damascus.

- The Photian Schism illustrates the complexities of Byzantine church politics and the growing differences between Byzantine and Roman expressions of Christianity and church.

- Middle Byzantine culture saw developments in monasticism, literature, liturgy, popular piety, art, and architecture that would characterize the Byzantine church from that period forward.

- Byzantine missionaries and missionaries from the Church of the

East established Christianity in Moravia, Bulgaria, Russia, Central Asia, China, India, Korea, and Japan.

- Heraclius promulgated the document *Ekthesis*, in order to promote Monotheletism.

- The Monothelete Syrian Christians of Lebanon were known as Maronites.

- The schism associated with the Patriarch Photius (858–67, 878–86) illustrates the deepening chasm between the Byzantine and Roman churches.

- The large cenobite community at Mt. Athos became the chief center of Orthodox monasticism.

Reflection Questions

1. Explain the rise and defeat of monotheletism, highlighting major players, crucial doctrines, and key events.

2. Explain the Photian Schism — its background and outcomes. What does the Schism say about the deep differences between Eastern and Western expressions of Christianity?

3. Describe the major features of Middle Byzantine culture, especially as they pertain to the church.

Discussion Question

1. Discuss the backgrounds, circumstances, and outcomes of the sixth and seventh ecumenical councils.

Quiz

1. (T/F) Nicaea II made a clear distinction between "honorable reverence" of pictures and "true devotion" to God.

2. (T/F) The Church of the East brought Christianity to the Chinese imperial court by the seventh century.

3. (T/F) Islam initially pressured Christians to convert.

4. (T/F) Many Christians welcomed the Muslims as a liberating force from the Byzantine emperor.

5. (T/F) Middle Byzantine church buildings conveyed a strong sense of movement upward, from earth to heaven.

6. (T/F) The Eastern church differed from Roman Catholic missions in allowing new churches to organize themselves on racial and national lines.

7. Who wrote the classic defense of icon veneration?

    a) Pope Honorius
    b) Maximus the Confessor
    c) Simeon the New Theologian
    d) John of Damascus

8. The Paulicians are especially associated with what country?

    a) Bulgaria
    b) Lebanon
    c) Armenia
    d) Egypt

9. What was the first stage in the Christian response to Islam?

    a) To see Islam as a chastisement for Christians' sins
    b) To engage Islam in serious polemics
    c) To translate Muslim works into Greek
    d) To advance an apocalyptic interpretation of Islam

10. Who was the founder of Russian Christianity?

    a) Vladimir
    b) Queen Olga
    c) Methodius
    d) Cyril

ANSWER KEY

1. T, 2. T, 3. F, 4. T, 5. F, 6. T, 7. D, 8. C, 9. A, 10. A

CHAPTER 18

The Western Church from the Seventh to Ninth Centuries

You Should Know

- In the clash between Celtic and Roman styles of Christian expression, a hybrid form emerged, loyal to Rome and Roman forms yet retaining many elements of the Celtic spirit.

- Missionary-monks from Ireland and England helped restore, reform, and expand the church on the European continent.

- The reign of Charlemagne and the Carolingian dynasty marked a season of relative peace and stability for much of Western Europe, with significant developments in Christian expansion, church-state relations, Benedictine monasticism, scholarship, theology, and church organization.

- By the ninth century, Christian ritual and belief was coming to pervade the daily lives of many in medieval Europe, though various non-Christian elements persisted.

- The Carolingian period saw a number of theological controversies, including debates about predestination, the Eucharist, the *filioque*, and religious art.

- In the seventh–ninth centuries, the papacy moved decisively towards a papal monarchy, and the groundwork was laid for the medieval synthesis of church and state.

- *Pseudo-Isidorian Decretals*: a collection of materials that became the basis of the claims for papal monarchy in the Middle Ages

- Canonical clergy at cathedrals served parish responsibilities in the world but lived according to a rule.

- Ninian: the "apostle of Scotland"

Reflection Questions

1. Compare and contrast Celtic and Roman styles of mission and church in the early Middle Ages.

2. What strategies were used to convert and Christianize people in Western Europe in the seventh–ninth centuries?

3. Describe two major theological controversies that occurred in the Carolingian Empire in the seventh–ninth centuries. Explain the backgrounds, major players, points at issue, and results.

Discussion Question

1. In your estimation, what were the most crucial factors in the construction of the foundation for medieval Europe that was laid in the seventh–ninth centuries? Substantiate your answer with reference to persons, events, developments, and any other data you find necessary to explain your answer.

Quiz

1. (T/F) Papal authority was the main issue debated in the Synod of Whitby (664).

2. (T/F) Charlemagne had Augustine's *City of God* read to him each night.

3. (T/F) The monastic model of John Cassian became standard throughout the Carolingian kingdom.

4. (T/F) The British bishops were impressed by Augustine of Canterbury's humility when they met.

5. (T/F) In the Carolingian period, bishops were named by the king, and ecclesiastical dioceses were determined by agreement between the state and the pope.

6. (T/F) Baptism by affusion came to replace baptism by immersion in the medieval Western church.

7. Who wrote the first doctrinal treatise on the Lord's Supper, arguing for a realistic identification of the elements with Jesus's body and blood?

   a) Alcuin
   b) Radbertus
   c) Gottschalk
   d) Ratramnus

8. Who succeeded in gaining the patronage of kings and popes in his efforts to reform churches and convert pagans in eighth-century Europe?

   a) Columbanus
   b) Winfrid (Boniface)
   c) Aidan
   d) Willibrord (Clement)

9. What were the *Libri Carolini* written to address?

   a) Double predestination
   b) The "Adoptionist" controversy
   c) The *filioque* clause
   d) The use of religious art in worship

10. Which of the following was NOT typical of early Celtic Christianity?

    a) Organization by parish and diocese
    b) Missionary zeal
    c) Identified Christian life with penance
    d) Associated with clan life

CHAPTER 19

Decline and Renewal of Vitality in the West

The Ninth to the Eleventh Centuries

You Should Know

- After a period of marked decline in the ninth and tenth centuries, revival in the institutions of monasticism, the imperial office, and the papacy set the stage in the eleventh century for the medieval synthesis.

- The Norse and Viking invasions disequilibrated medieval culture, though the invaders were converted and Christianized in the tenth and eleventh centuries.

- Church structures, especially the papacy, descended more deeply into feudalism during the ninth and tenth centuries.

- Largely as a result of its autonomy from feudal structures, the monastery of Cluny was able to promote a sweeping reform of monasticism, thereby transforming the church's impact on the society of the late tenth and eleventh centuries.

- Imperial power passed from the Franks to the German Ottonian dynasty, key representatives of which supported church reform.

- Reform-minded monarchs supported the installation of reforming popes such as Leo III, who transformed the papacy and helped lift it out of its feudal entanglements.

- During an era when reforms in the Western church supported an independent papacy, tensions with the Eastern church came to a head in the controversy between Pope Leo IX and Patriarch Michael Cerularius, resulting in the Great Schism of 1054.

- Simony: the practice of paying money in order to receive a clerical benefice
- Nicolaitanism: the practice of married clergy called by the Cluniacs
- Leo IX: the great reforming pope of the eleventh century

Reflection Questions

1. Describe the story of papal decline and renewal in the ninth to eleventh centuries, highlighting key players and significant events.

2. Explain the eleventh-century monastic, imperial, and papal revivals, in terms of their background, interconnections, and major players.

3. What impact did the monastery of Cluny have on the church and medieval culture?

Discussion Question

1. Why did the Great Schism of 1054 happen? Explain the background to the division and describe the specific circumstances of the eleventh-century events.

Quiz

1. (T/F) After a period of "dark ages," the eleventh century saw institutional revival.

2. (T/F) During much of the tenth and eleventh centuries the Roman aristocracy was controlled by the papacy.

3. (T/F) Otto I cultivated alliances with dukes and nobles in order to secure local authority against bishops and abbots.

4. (T/F) Many monasteries placed themselves under the abbot of Cluny.

5. (T/F) Pope Leo IX sought to preserve Italian control of the College of Cardinals.

6. (T/F) The people of Rome granted Henry III the right to choose Rome's bishop.

7. What characteristic of the monastery of Cluny was most significant in making it a powerful agent of reform?

    a) Its autonomy
    b) Canonical clergy
    c) Support of the Ottonian kings
    d) The "Peace of God"

8. Who acted as the pope's agent in excommunicating Michael Cerularius and his associates?

    a) Constantine X
    b) Hildebrand
    c) Peter Damian
    d) Humbert

9. The "Truce of God" provided for what limitations on warfare and feuding?

    a) The outlawing of combat between Christians
    b) The restriction of fighting to certain seasons
    c) Only kings and popes could declare war
    d) Non-combatants and clergy were not to be attacked

10. What Bohemian duke enthusiastically promoted Christianity on his half-pagan realm in the early tenth century?

    a) Olaf
    b) Willibrord
    c) Wenceslas
    d) Stephen I

ANSWER KEY
1. T, 2. F, 3. F, 4. T, 5. F, 6. T, 7. A, 8. D, 9. B, 10. C

CHAPTER 20

The Papal Reform Movement and the First Crusade

You Should Know

- The papal revival of the eleventh century climaxed in the papacy of Gregory VII.

- Conflict over lay investiture became the defining issue, expressing competing views of kingship and the proper relationship between church and state.

- Numerous factors help explain the significance of the conflict between King Henry IV of Germany and Pope Gregory VII over lay investiture, including the imperial and papal revivals, the church's entanglement in feudalism, and politics in Germany and Italy.

- Through a display of penance, Henry IV gained a tactical victory over Gregory VII, but the papacy won the moral victory in securing the symbol of imperial humility before the pope.

- Multiple factors played into the development of the First Crusade, including the evolution of penance, changing views about the church's role in warfare, the influence of Islam, the practice of pilgrimage, and a desire to reunite the church.

- Pope Urban II responded to the Byzantine emperor's pleas for help by preaching the First Crusade, offering papal indulgences to crusaders, and helping mobilize French nobles to lead the armies.

- Although the First Crusade contributed to the deterioration of many relationships, the capture of select targets brought western military rule to the Holy Land for a period. Knightly monastic orders arose to protect the conquered lands and safeguard pilgrims.

- The essential parts of medieval penance were contrition, confession, and (works of) satisfaction.

- Indulgence: remission of the temporal punishment of sin

- Urban II: the pope who preached the First Crusade

Reflection Questions

1. How did the investiture controversy come to be a crucial moment in the history of the papacy and the medieval church?

2. Explain the conflict between Gregory VII and Henry IV, highlighting the political and ecclesial factors and describing the outcomes of the conflict.

3. What factors came together to trigger the First Crusade? What were the results of the Crusades?

Discussion Question

1. Compare and contrast the attitudes responsible for the launching of the Crusades with those of Christians of earlier periods, illustrating by means of persons, sources, and events.

Quiz

1. (T/F) Alongside chastity, obedience, and warfare, the Knights Templar emphasized poverty most of all.

2. (T/F) The conflict between Gregory VII and Henry IV was essentially a disagreement over two competing views of kingship.

3. (T/F) The Copts in Egypt welcomed the crusaders as liberators.

4. (T/F) Since Carolingian times, penance twice a year at Lent and Christmas had become the norm.

5. (T/F) In the eleventh century, killing a person was a grievous sin, even in a battle approved by the pope.

6. (T/F) At the Diet of Worms, Henry IV showed penance by walking barefoot in the snow.

7. What was the title of Gregory VII's summary statement of papal authorities?

   a) *Dictatus papae*
   b) *Index librorum prohibitorum*
   c) *Decretum*
   d) *Deus le volt*

8. What marked the final settlement in the investiture controversy?

   a) The Council of Clermont
   b) Henry IV's display of penance
   c) The Concordat of Worms
   d) Ivo of Chartres's formulation of canons

9. What social expectation strongly impacted the conflict between Henry IV and Gregory VII?

   a) Indulgences
   b) Feudalism
   c) Proprietary churches
   d) Commutations

10. What leader of the First Crusade took the title of Lord Protector of Jerusalem?

   a) Godfrey
   b) Baldwin
   c) Raymond
   d) Bohemond

CHAPTER 21

Intellectual Revival
The Rise of Scholasticism

You Should Know

- The twelfth century saw an intellectual revival in medieval culture and the Western church, based on the kind of teaching and learning that occurred in cathedral schools.

- Scholasticism was based on confidence in human reason and used a dialectical method of disputation to engage authorities and arguments in order to resolve problems, particularly those connected to the philosophical question of universals.

- Scholastic methods and changing positions on the question of universals transformed the ways scholars engaged and debated such doctrines as the Eucharist, the incarnation, the church, and the atonement.

- Anselm of Canterbury and Peter Abelard are the most significant representatives of early Scholasticism, whose work and teaching shaped the assumptions, aims, and methods of intellectual inquiry in western culture for centuries.

- Anselm's treatise *Proslogion* presented his famous ontological argument for God.

- Scholasticism placed a high degree of confidence in reason.

- A debate about the use of the new scholastic methods in explaining the Trinity was triggered by the views of Roscellinus, the founder of Nominalism.

Reflection Questions

1. What was the problem of universals, as engaged by Scholasticism, and how did the discussions impact Christian doctrine in the eleventh and twelfth centuries?

2. What were the most popular theories of the atonement in the early twelfth century? Explain the theories and give their proponents.

3. Discuss the circumstances, issues, and major players in the second eucharistic controversy. How did the results of the controversy affect church doctrine and liturgical practice?

Discussion Question

1. Explain Scholasticism, in terms of its assumptions, methods, content, and form, illustrating with reference to a particular theological discussion of the eleventh or twelfth century. How were these assumptions, methods, and results similar to those of the early church fathers? How were they different?

Quiz

1. (T/F) The development of the doctrine of transubstantiation led to the common practice of offering the Eucharist in both kinds to the laity.

2. (T/F) Anselm sought to demonstrate the propositions of faith on the basis of reason alone.

3. (T/F) The scholasticus Berengar formulated the doctrine of transubstantiation.

4. (T/F) *Cur deus homo* presented the atonement theory that eventually won the largest following.

5. (T/F) Abelard argued that motives, however well-intended, play no role in determining whether behavior is right or wrong.

6. (T/F) Nearly all the scholastic thinkers had an element of mysticism in them.

7. In scholastic method, what term corresponds best to the process of stating arguments for and against a problem?

    a) *Sententia*
    b) *Disputatio*
    c) *Sic et non*
    d) *Quaestio*

8. Which position on universals sees them not as real, but helpful inferences drawn from observation?

    a) Moderate realism
    b) Nominalism
    c) Extreme realism
    d) Nominal conceptualism

9. Which scholar held that he had to doubt in order to know?

    a) Anselm
    b) Berengar
    c) Abelard
    d) Bernard

10. Which scholar is known for the moral-exemplary theory of the atonement?

    a) Anselm
    b) Berengar
    c) Abelard
    d) Bernard

CHAPTER 22

Monastic, Literary, Political, and Cultural Activities in the Twelfth Century

You Should Know

- Church reform and renewal in the twelfth century was triggered largely by increased monastic vitality and new expressions of monasticism, the most influential of which was the Cistercian reform of Benedictine monasticism.

- The Cistercian leader Bernard of Clairvaux was the guiding spiritual influence of the age.

- A lasting synthesis between the monastic spirituality of Bernard and the dialectic methods of Abelard was achieved through the work of such luminaries as Hugh of St. Victor and Peter Lombard.

- Romanesque style combined Roman and Byzantine features with local elements, to shape the Christian art and architecture of the tenth through twelfth centuries.

- A growing preoccupation with saints, their sites, and their relics — and especially Mary — shaped the popular piety of western Christianity, along with developments in music and poetry.

- Rhythms of competition, antagonism, and cooperation continued to characterize church-state relations in the twelfth century, most evident in the relations between the papacy and emerging national monarchies. The Third Crusade was a failed expression of the impulse to cooperate.

- Key developments occurred in the national Eastern churches in the eleventh and twelfth centuries.

- The canonist (John) Gratian composed the Decretum, which became the standard sourcebook for studying and practicing canon law.

- Hildegard of Bingen was a twelfth-century abbess who preached her prophetic visions of judgment.

Reflection Questions

1. What role did monastic movements play in the Western church and society in the twelfth century? Illustrate with reference to significant leaders and influential movements.

2. Describe the main themes of Romanesque style, illustrating with reference to medieval art architecture.

3. What expressions of personal piety dominated the Western church in the twelfth century?

Discussion Question

1. Compare and contrast the work and impact of Bernard of Clairvaux, Hugh of St. Victor, and Peter Lombard.

Quiz

1. (T/F) Converts to monasticism and the establishment of monasteries increased in the eleventh and twelfth centuries.

2. (T/F) Lombard's *Book of Sentences* became the standard medieval theology textbook.

3. (T/F) Jewish and Arabic scholars in Europe lagged far behind the Christian intellectual revival of the twelfth century.

4. (T/F) The official doctrine of purgatory was formulated by Hugh of St. Victor.

5. (T/F) Bernard of Clairvaux promoted the Second Crusade.

6. (T/F) In the twelfth century, the popes began to allow other bishops to canonize saints.

7. Which new monastic movement emphasized the need to return to the simplicity of Benedictine monasticism?

   a) Cistercians
   b) Carthusians
   c) Premonstratensians
   d) Augustinian Canons

8. Who fixed the number of sacraments at seven?

   a) Thomas Becket
   b) Hugh of St. Victor
   c) John Gratian
   d) Peter Lombard

9. Who brought together the priorities and methods of both Bernard of Clairvaux and Abelard in his work?

   a) John of Salisbury
   b) Hugh of St. Victor
   c) Bruno of Rheims
   d) John Gratian

10. What major participant in the Third Crusade drowned crossing a river?

   a) Philip II Augustus
   b) Saladin
   c) Frederick I Barbarossa
   d) Richard I the Lion-Hearted

CHAPTER 23

The Glory of the Western Medieval Church
The Thirteenth Century

You Should Know

- The papacy of Innocent III marked the peak of papal power in the Middle Ages.

- The mendicant orders represented the latest wave of ascetic renewal in the thirteenth century, expressed in the careers of Dominic and Francis of Assisi, and in the priorities and impact of the movements they started.

- The intellectual revival of the eleventh and twelfth centuries culminated in the development in the thirteenth of the universities, a third force in Christendom alongside the empire and the priesthood.

- The career and legacy of the Dominican Thomas Aquinas constitute the crowning achievement of medieval Scholasticism; his project to synthesize Christian theology and Aristotelian thought was singularly influential in western Christian intellectual history.

- The Franciscan order produced scholars who preserved Augustinian emphases on divine illumination, mysticism, and love, providing a counterpoint to Aquinas: Bonaventure, Roger Bacon, and Duns Scotus.

- In the thinking of Duns Scotus, the will is primary to intelligence, in both God and humans.

- The Gothic art and architecture of the period emphasized harmony, verticality, space, and luminosity.

- *Books of Hours*: often lavishly illuminated works that gave devotions for daily times of prayer for laypersons

- *Summa Theologiae*: Thomas Aquinas's great systematic theology

- The Fourth Lateran Council made annual confession and communion obligatory.

Reflection Questions

1. Explain the rise and development of the papacy from the period of the early church until the papacy of Innocent III. Why is the papacy of Innocent III often considered as representing the peak of papal power?

2. Compare and contrast the persons of Dominic and Francis of Assisi. How do their differences express themselves in the different priorities, missions, and impact of their orders?

3. Describe the rise of universities as a "third force" in Christendom.

Discussion Question

1. Compare and contrast the theological projects of Thomas Aquinas and Bonaventure. Explain the basic elements of Aquinas's project to synthesize Aristotelian thought and Christian theology, illustrating by reference to his work.

Quiz

1. (T/F) In the thirteenth century, images of Jesus on the cross changed from realistic depictions of his agony to depictions of his exalted reign over sin and the world.

2. (T/F) The Dominicans emphasized scholarship and combating heresy.

3. (T/F) The availability of the entire corpus of Plato was a major factor in the development of medieval culture in the thirteenth century.

4. (T/F) Thomas Aquinas insisted that all knowledge may be known by reason, and that revelation is necessary only for the unlearned.

5. (T/F) Francis of Assisi would not condone the drawing up of a formal rule to govern his followers.

6. (T/F) Gothic depictions of final judgment emphasized the hope of salvation more than Romanesque ones had done.

7. What was the first example of the new Gothic style of architecture?
   a) Cathedral of Notre Dame
   b) Abbey church at St. Denis
   c) Sainte-Chapelle
   d) Cathedral of Chartres

8. Which pope placed England under the interdict due to conflict over the appointment of Stephen Langton?
   a) Honorius III
   b) Alexander III
   c) Innocent III
   d) Gregory IX

9. Which scholar stressed the importance of divine illumination in the quest for truth?
   a) Bonaventure
   b) Roger Bacon
   c) Thomas Aquinas
   d) Albertus Magnus

10. What became a third force in the thirteenth century, alongside the *imperium* and the *sacerdotium*?

   a) The papacy
   b) Universities
   c) Mendicant orders
   d) Religious lay movements

CHAPTER 24

Portents of Decline

You Should Know

- In the face of diminishing popular confidence in the structures of the church, numerous lay religious movements arose in the twelfth and thirteenth centuries, prompting the Roman Catholic Church to attempt various measures of control, including the Inquisition.

- The church and medieval structures of power struggled to cope with diverse religious elements in society, including Jews, the Cathari, expressions of vernacular theology such as the women's Beguine movement, and expressions of female mysticism.

- In the face of the Mongol conquests, the missions and vitality of the church in central Asia and China was sharply reduced.

- The Second Council of Lyons met in 1274, ostensibly to further a project of reunion between West and East, but without lasting results.

- Effective pastoral care and worship were in serious decline in the thirteenth century, as eschatological speculation and fanaticism increased.

- The poet and Florentine magistrate Dante Alighieri went on a pilgrimage to Rome in 1300 and wrote the most significant literary expression of the medieval worldview.

- In terms of its claims, the papacy of Boniface VIII marks the pinnacle of the development of medieval papal theory; in terms of actual effectiveness in the face of emerging national monarchies, it marks a period of grave decline.

- Cathari/Albigensians: a people group that held to a dualist understanding of the world and religion and were targeted for a crusade

- The papal bull *Unam sanctam* of 1302: summarized medieval papal theory and made extravagant claims for papal authority

Reflection Questions

1. Explain the rise of lay religious movements and vernacular theology in the thirteenth century, illustrating with reference to the background and key leaders. How did the church respond?

2. Compare and contrast the Waldenses, Cathari, and Beguines, both with respect to their chief characteristics and the church's responses.

3. In what ways does the papacy of Boniface VIII represent a significant point in the development of the medieval papacy?

Discussion Question

1. Discuss the Council of Lyons (1274): Why did it occur? Who were the chief players? What were its main outcomes?

Quiz

1. (T/F) Peter John Olivi advocated the doctrine of papal infallibility as a way of limiting papal power.

2. (T/F) Kublai Khan asked the pope to send a hundred Christian teachers to his kingdom.

3. (T/F) Abuses in the Inquisition were more with individuals and the way it was carried out than with the system itself.

4. (T/F) In response to the church's emphasis on celibacy, Peter Valdes stressed the importance of marriage as a spiritual practice.

5. (T/F) Thomas Aquinas represented the Western theological position at the Council of Lyons (1274).

6. (T/F) Miracle and morality plays in the vernacular were banned in the thirteenth century by papal decree.

7. Who presented a theory of the Trinitarian periodization of history?

   a) Gregory bar Hebraeus
   b) Peter de Bruys
   c) Stephen Tempier
   d) Joachim of Fiore

8. What thirteenth-century leader converted the idea of Christian empire into imperialism?

   a) Gregory X
   b) Louis IX
   c) Charles of Anjou
   d) Genghis Khan

9. Who promoted missions to Muslims and Jews by means of preaching and martyrdom?

   a) Joachim of Fiore
   b) Raymond Lull
   c) Dionysius bar Salibi
   d) Prester John

10. What female mystic was burned at the stake for heresy?

   a) Margaret of Porette
   b) Mechthild of Magdeburg
   c) Gertrude of Helfta
   d) Elizabeth of Hungary and Thuringia

Notes